GLEE CLUB™

GLEE CLUB
STYLE
CHOOSING COSTUMES,
MAKEUP, SETS, AND PROPS

COLLEEN RYCKERT COOK

ROSEN
PUBLISHING®

NEW YORK

Published in 2013 by The Rosen Publishing Group, Inc.
29 East 21st Street, New York, NY 10010

Copyright © 2013 by The Rosen Publishing Group, Inc.

First Edition

Library of Congress Cataloging-in-Publication Data

Cook, Colleen Ryckert.
Glee club style: choosing costumes, makeup, sets, and props/Colleen Ryckert Cook.—1st ed.
    p. cm.—(Glee club)
Includes bibliographical references and index.
ISBN 978-1-4488-6876-6 (library binding)—ISBN 978-1-4488-6883-4 (pbk.)—ISBN 978-1-4488-6884-1 (6-pack)
1. Glee clubs. I. Title.
MT930.C67 2013
792.02–dc23
                                                    2011048594

Manufactured in the United States of America

CPSIA Compliance Information: Batch #S12YA: For further information, contact Rosen Publishing, New York, New York, at 1-800-237-9932.

CONTENTS

INTRODUCTION

The curtains part to reveal twenty, thirty, even forty or more bodies on the stage. Something glitters in the spotlight—perhaps the strap of an evening gown or the silver handle of a cane in a young man's hand. The music starts, and arms and voices rise in unison. Then, bodies are in motion, gliding effortlessly across the stage in a choreographed dance, singing their hearts out. Emotions explode from their faces and voices.

It looks like the opening number from a Broadway musical. But it's not happening at the Gershwin Theater. Instead, these performers are taking over high school stages across America.

It's the new glee club.

Thanks to the Fox hit show *Glee*, the newest fans don't picture the all-male clubs of yore. Both young and old, these fans picture glee club as what is called show choir in many schools: male and female students singing well-known—and

Student choirs and choruses have been around since the 1700s. Modern student singing groups still perform traditional choir music, but high school show choirs take it up a notch with choreography, costumes, and stage sets.

sometimes not so well-known—songs that feature group choruses and lead vocalists, costumes and sets, storytelling and vocal emotion, and, most of all, choreography.

It isn't your mama's jazz hands either. Today's show choirs incorporate hip-hop, swing, acrobatics, tumbling—you name it, a show choir has tried it.

All kinds of students are finding themselves eager to join in the dancing and singing. Music lets you express your personal creativity, joy, and frustration. And mostly it's out and out fun. You play with a song to create something new and real. More and more, students in high schools that haven't offered glee clubs since the 1960s are starting their own—such as the young men and women at Johns Creek High School in Johns Creek, Georgia, who started a glee club in 2010 and posted their videos on YouTube to drum up awareness.

Like any extracurricular activity, joining glee club or show choir involves extra expenses. These costs can get high if you join a competitive group that travels or performs in elaborate costumes. Fees range from around $100 a year for a basic performing shirt and shoes to $2,500 or more for highly competitive groups to cover performance costs, as well as transportation and hotel for competitions. There might be extra fees for tuxedo rentals or suits for men. Women may need to purchase one or more dresses, hosiery, undergarments, specific makeup kits and hair products, and jewelry.

This book will offer ideas on starting up or building participation in your own singing club, including ways to create inexpensive costumes and sets for unforgettable performances.

CHAPTER 1

GLEEFUL COSTUMES

The first impression an audience gets of a glee club is the singers' costumes. Before the music starts, before the voices rise, the audience sees a group onstage. What a glee club chooses to wear signals the kind of performance an audience can expect. That's why it's so important to put a lot of thought into costume choices.

The best costumes are easy to move in and create a cohesive look. These are the two qualities to keep in mind when choosing the outfits your glee club members will wear. Glee club and show choir singers move about the stage performing sometimes complex choreography while trying to hit all the right notes.

You don't want restrictive costumes that strangle movement. The last thing any singer wants during a performance is to struggle to lift arms overhead, wiggle out of a wedgie, or worry about "wardrobe malfunctions." Imagine a troupe of singers huffing and panting through a song. It's hard enough for many first-timers to simultaneously sing their hearts out and hit all the dance steps at the right time. Throw in a few lifts or a series of tricky footwork, and their jobs become ten times harder if they can't move smoothly.

That isn't to say baggy is better, unless it makes sense for the song. The costumes should enhance the vocal performance, not detract from it.

Bear in mind that glee clubs attract a wide range of people who love to sing and perform. Whenever people gather in large groups, you will find a range of body types. Pick styles that are suitable for teenagers that may be as young as fourteen years old and their varied sizes, with plenty of room for wide arm gestures and the flexibility to bend or kick easily.

The Basic Uniform

Some glee clubs forego elaborate costumes and instead choose a specific look for all their performances. These can range from a simple performance T-shirt or polo-style shirt worn with jeans and tennis shoes to tuxedos and floor-length evening dresses.

Find choices that flatter all body types and still remain comfortable. For a more formal look, choose dark suits or jackets and dress pants with button-down shirts and ties for men. You can always play with the colors of the shirts, ties, and even vests or cummerbunds. For women, flowing knee-length

Costumes give an audience its first clue about a choir's personality. Some go with traditional evening dresses and tuxedoes; others choose theatrical clothes that reflect the song's energy or topic. What matters most is consistency.

dresses work well and keep the body free to move. Some groups choose two-piece outfits so that they can alternate different tops and bottoms and still keep that unified look. In general, A-line dresses with flared skirts flatter all body types. The A-line design minimizes both heavier middles and hips, and the flared skirt makes a lovely silhouette as a dancer moves across the stage.

Halter-top styles and sweetheart necklines also look great on most body shapes, plus they draw the eye upward to the singer's face. Black dress shoes for men and low-heeled sandals or pumps finish the dressier look, and boys and girls can still dance easily with practice.

LONG LIVE GLEE

Glee clubs have been a singing tradition in many colleges since the mid-nineteenth century. The oldest is the Harvard Glee Club, founded in 1858. Rounding out the top nine of the longest-lived glee clubs are:

- University of Michigan Men's Glee Club, founded in 1859
- Yale Glee Club, founded in 1861
- University of Pennsylvania Glee Club, founded in 1862
- Amherst College Glee Club, founded in 1865
- Cornell University Glee Club, founded in 1868
- Virginia Glee Club, founded in 1871
- Rutgers University Glee Club, founded in 1872
- Princeton Glee Club, founded in 1874
- Penn State Glee Club, founded in 1888

Of these, only the Yale Glee Club and the Princeton Glee Club are coed. The rest remain the traditional all-male choir. Most of these universities also have mixed choirs and even show choirs.

Sturdier fabrics are also kinder to the less-than-perfect bodies most of us have. Fabrics that cling too closely to the body and certain shiny materials, such as lamé, can distract from the performance. It's better to embellish smaller bits of an outfit, such as straps, cuffs, or belts.

Casual groups can get away with khaki pants and polo shirts in school colors, or even a variety of colors if the styles are similar enough. Some glee clubs prefer to perform in athletic shoes.

Most of all, choose costumes that are age appropriate.

The female singers and dancers on the television show *Glee* might appear in plunging necklines and clinging skirts and shorts for their skits, but most teenagers will feel self-conscious rather than confident if the getup is too indiscreet. Who needs to worry about accidently exposing too much when hitting a high note or doing a high kick?

Play Dress Up

In central Ohio, members of Olentangy High School's show choir, Keynotes, often dress uniformly, with the girls wearing the same knee-length dress and shoes and the men in suits, shoes, and sometimes even spats. But the costumes for their 2009 spring show, which featured songs from the Broadway musical *Jersey Boys*, were decidedly more individual. The unifying theme was a 1960s feel, complete with retro dresses and beehives for the girls and two-tone jackets and pencil ties for the boys.

Yes, they looked and sounded great onstage. But a glee club doesn't necessarily need to spend a lot of money making elaborate period costumes to go along with songs. Pick a theme for your performance, then think about a simple unifying piece of clothing or accessory. Make it as simple as picking one item almost everyone has in their closet—say a hoodie, or even jeans—and build from that. The costumes don't necessarily have to be identical, just cohesive and united.

Immaculate Conception Academy for girls in Manila, Philippines, performed a *Mama Mia!* medley wearing a colorful mix of clothing styles. The girls' outfits likely came from their own closets. Some wore wide skirts and loose tops, others leggings and tunics. They all wore flat-heeled shoes. The

Pop and Broadway songs are staples in most show choirs' repertoires. A theatrical costume, such as this 1960s look for a choir's tribute to the Broadway hit *Showgirls*, can turn a great vocal performance into high-impact magic.

style mimicked the low-key Greek isle feel of the movie and Broadway play's setting. It was a vibrant performance that matched the mood of the songs.

Keep It Simple

The Classics from Wheaton Warrenville High School in Wheaton, Illinois, won the FAME National Show Choir Championships in 2011. Their costumes were lovely and perfect for the song, but they always choose a simple, unified look compared to some other choirs in their competitive league. This dress style is easy for the girls to move in. The boys wear matching suits, ties, and shoes. Instead of visual drama, the Classics director, John Burlace, focused on vocal drama. Choreographer Dwight Jordan staged elaborate dance steps that incorporated the entire body. It was likely akin to running a marathon while singing a medley of Lady Gaga—exhausting. The Classics made it look like a cakewalk.

New show choirs likely don't have the bank accounts to stage elaborate concept performances with multiple costume changes or afford even the simpler designs favored by Wheaton Warrenville. Simple dress can be just as effective with a powerful vocal performance.

Black, white, and red are bold choices that can look dramatic onstage. Some of the best looks are also the easiest to pull off. Start with a solid foundation: black pants, leggings, skirt, or dress. Throw on a black T-shirt or loose blouse. Most teens have something black in their closets, and putting their personality into the performance can make the show stronger. The costumes become a blank palette.

Next, add some color—a white or red pencil tie, scarf, vest, hat, belt, or other accessory. Or make it sparkling gold, or even a rainbow. Pick a variety of colors. Have fun, and let each singer's personality shine through.

Keep It Fresh

One of the most powerful performances on *Glee* was the football team performing Beyoncé's "All the Single Ladies."

THE FIRST "GLEE"

Glee (noun). 1. Jubilant delight; joy. 2. a type of song for male voices, often sung in three or four parts.

For millions of self-proclaimed "gleeks", "glee" means the New Directions singing group from Fox's hit show *Glee*. For some, that was their first introduction to glee clubs.

Glee clubs have been around for more than two hundred years. Male singers at the Harrow School in London, England, in 1787 were the first troupe to call themselves a "glee club." They focused on singing those short part songs for male voices known as glees. Glee clubs remained popular for the next hundred years. Choral societies, which sang a broader repertoire, eventually replaced them in popularity in the United Kingdom.

Across the Atlantic, however, glees were becoming more and more popular on campuses. One hundred years after Harrow's first glee club, hundreds of glee clubs were singing on university and college stages across America. Today, there are still dozens of active traditional glee clubs at American universities.

The juxtaposition of hulking football players in full pads and helmets who break out into dance and song right before the game-determining final play made the performance explode with a new energy. It was so much more entertaining than the obvious choice of women in black leotards and heels.

And that is the key: pass over the obvious staging and go with an unexpected twist. No need for elaborate lighting or flash and glitter to make a huge impression. Onstage in real life, it would have been just as fun had it been girls wearing skate pads and hard hats, or the boys singing to the girls instead, with choreography to match the switcheroo.

Greece Athena High School in Rochester, New York, staged

Costumes add flair and drama onstage, but they might be the wrong kind if singers can't move easily in them. Straps must be sturdy and secure to avoid potential wardrobe malfunctions. You'll also want fabric that's easy to clean.

a performance of "Defying Gravity" from the Broadway hit *Wicked* using a brilliant costume choice. The soloist emerged from backstage walking slowing in a gown. Her skirt was unbelievably long and dragging across the stage floor. As she hit the chorus, she suddenly rose into the air. Fellow choir members had slipped under the skirt to lift her. Other singers grasped the edges of her skirt and pulled it out into a wide bell. The group then slowly turned in circles, members raising and lowering the skirt hem in rhythm to her song. At the end she returned back to earth, gravity-bound again.

Keep It Affordable

Do the prices found in show choir catalogs leave you feeling downhearted? Dress prices can range from $99 to $350 or more apiece. A large enough group can get decent bulk pricing, but this isn't always economical for startup or smaller groups. When budgets are tight, glee singers get creative.

It's easy to garnish simple, affordable pieces such as white T-shirts or hoodies, jeans, or even skullcaps. A trip to the local craft shop can get ideas rolling. Glitter, puff paint, BeDazzlers, and iron-ons can stretch as far as your imagination goes.

Other options for cash-strapped clubs include renting, or shopping if they ever unload old costumes, from local theater groups or junior college departments. Or work out deals with your home economics or fashion design teachers. Their students can sew from patterns or even help design unique looks. Share the expenses and everyone wins.

CHAPTER 2

MAKEUP

If you've ever been backstage in a theater during a performance, you likely thought you'd stepped into a freaky Halloween costume party. In the darkened seats of the auditorium or theater, the actors look perfectly normal onstage. But up close, out from under the bright lights, you see dark swaths of foundation lining mouth corners and under cheekbones, and white streaks above the cheekbone, along the nose, and under the eyes. The actors sport dark lipstick, thick eyeliner, a blanket of rouge, and false eyelashes that look like spiders on their lids. Even the men wear heavy mascara or trimmed-down false eyelashes, lipstick, eyeliner, and blush.

Pair up with a partner and give each other a makeover. It's a great way to figure out which makeup works best for a performance. Play with colors. Find the perfect amount of shadow. Then get under stage lights to evaluate the look.

If an actor is playing an older character, the makeup is even more dramatic, with drawn-in dark gray lines to mimic wrinkles around the eyes and mouth.

Sure, you might think that actors in a play need that heavy makeup because they are performing characters. But glee club singers aren't characters. They are themselves. They don't need to look different. Why would they need to apply their makeup this way, so heavily and so dark?

If you've never performed onstage or even in front of a crowd, you might not realize just how much bright lights can wash out facial features. Lights can also accent the wrong parts of a face, such as making eyes look like there are massive black circles under them. Try this experiment. Go into a brightly lit room. Ask a friend to shine a flashlight in your face and then take a picture. Can you see all the colors of your eyes? The distinct shape of your nose? Even your mouth nearly disappears. Now hold the flashlight on top of your head and take a picture. How do those shadows look? Pretty funky, right?

That's what it looks like when a bare face is seen on the stage, with powerful lights shining down. Every detail gets washed out.

THE EVOLUTION OF AMERICAN GLEE

Historically, glee clubs were all-male choruses that sang brief ditties called glees—hence the name. The first U.S. college glee club formed in 1858 at Harvard University. Other clubs popped up at other universities, and by the twentieth century they were common at universities and high schools across the county. These men tended to wear tuxedos or other elegant clothes and sang a cappella or simple accompaniment on occasion.

In time a few clubs invited women to join, bringing a broader vocal range for more varied song styles. Soon longer pieces joined glees in the singers' concert lists. Glee clubs were staples for decades in American universities and high schools, and even middle schools, until a decline in popularity in the latter half of the twentieth century. Still, most high schools and colleges, and a small number of unaffiliated groups, kept the glee spirit going.

19

Veteran performers will tell you everyone needs makeup onstage or in front of a large crowd, and probably more than you realize. Boys as well as girls need stage makeup to stand out in the bright lights. In general, however, men look best without excessive or dramatic color unless makeup is necessary for a concept performance. Use flesh tones to accentuate what's there, not change a face or create something false. The first time you slap on the pancake, you might feel uncomfortable, but in time it will feel as normal as your own smile.

Natural Effects

Stage makeup must be heavy so that you don't wash out under bright lights, but that doesn't mean go garish with black eye shadows, brows, and lips unless the dramatic look is needed to enhance the song. Some songs and choreography might require those strong effects. John Burroughs High School in Burbank, California, performed a rendition of Falco's "Rock Me Amadeus" in pompadour wigs, Baroque costumes, white faces, and large black streaks on their eyes or cheeks. Their makeup and hair was dark and dramatic.

Depending on venue and your songs, you might be able to go lighter on the makeup. With another venue, you might find you need it heavier and darker.

So how do you know how much to use? Start light and add until you get the effect you want. Full dress rehearsals will let you know where you need to darken or lighten up your look. Flesh tones are always safe. Lighter tones will highlight light areas, such as the top of the nose, under eyebrows, and cheeks. Use a slightly darker tone to create contours under cheekbones, along the temples, and near the jawline. Blusher on the apples of everyone's cheeks, even the boys, will keep the face looking natural and healthy.

PUNK GLEE: THE BLUE RIBBON GLEE CLUB

The Blue Ribbon Glee Club is a Chicago-area singing club made up of anywhere from twenty to thirty singers. They started in an attic in 2007, a group of punk and alternative rock fans who wanted to make music together but weren't exactly into the whole band thing. They started performing punk songs a cappella at local venues, featuring songs from such bands as the Dead Kennedys, the Flaming Lips, and even heavy metal band Black Sabbath. In time, they built a reputation and a following.

The Blue Ribbon Glee Club keeps it simple. No elaborate instrumentals. They might have drums, a simple bass line, and occasional other percussions, but in general they let their voices do the work. Costumes are equally low maintenance. Everyone wears something in a similar color theme, usually casual. The only thing resembling an official uniform is the satin sash members don for some performances.

They also keep it clearly comfortable. Their dance moves are simple, if you can even call it dance. Members sway in rhythm to their voices. They might jump around in random bursts during the Fugazi song "Waiting Room," but mostly their voices have all the fun.

The Eyes Have It

Eyes, they say, are windows to the soul. They are the part of the face people focus on the most when talking to others. When watching a performance, people still look to the eyes of the person onstage. It's unnerving to see a creature without eyes. That's why it's so important to make the eyes really stand out onstage.

First, all but those with the darkest, thickest eyebrows will need to use a dark pencil to fill in their brows. Eyebrows create a frame for the eyes. Next, use black mascara to darken

Use makeup to enhance a performer's natural features. Fair-skinned people will need a heavier hand to stand out under harsh stage lights, but don't go overboard into ghoulish—unless that look works best for the song, of course!

the lashes. Dark-haired males or those with lusher lashes might be able to get away with a quick single coat, but fair-haired boys or those with skimpier lashes will definitely need the extra help. All girls will need mascara or even false eyelashes, depending upon the song or performance goals. You don't need to look like you've glued feather dusters to your lids. You can trim them down to a manageable length.

Use eye shadow colors that flatter each singer's unique coloring. While many dance squads require their members to wear the same eye shadow colors, most glee and show choir groups want their singers' personalities to show through, even as they are trying to create a cohesive, united feel. Part of that comes from each singer looking his or her best in colors that complement him or her.

Line the eyes with black to make them stand out. Use darker neutral shadows to contour the skin of the lid and crease and lighter colors to highlight the bone just under the brow. Sweep the color wider than you would for real life to make the eyes visible from even the back of the theater. Some might put dark eye shadow along the lower lid as well.

Mouth to Mouth

As important as eyes are to the face, the mouth is crucial to the voice. Your lips, teeth, and tongue form the words. Even males need some amount of lip color to make the mouth stand out onstage.

For starters, line the lips using a pencil that matches the lipstick or lip gloss. If you can't find a perfect match, go a shade slightly lighter. A darker line might stand out too much,

A singer's mouth is his or her instrument. Makeup needs to make the mouth noticeable without looking clownish. Choose shades close to the performer's natural color. Outlining the lips defines the natural shape.

creating a clown-like appearance. You just want the pencil to define the mouth.

Next, apply color. Again, keep the color choice in the same family—peach, plum, red, pink—but choose colors that best suit the individual singer's color tone. Some male members might need a small amount of color as well. Use a small amount of color that most closely matches the boy's natural lip color. The color makes the mouth bright and frames the smile.

You might find that your lip will occasionally stick to your teeth. Stage performers sometimes rub a light coat of petroleum jelly on their teeth to prevent this. It also helps your teeth look even shinier in the lights.

Crowning Glory

You've got the makeup down. What about hair? Again, the song can on occasion determine the hairstyle, but in general well-groomed hair pulled away from the singer's face is best. The audience wants to see the joy and expression of the singer. Headbands or ponytails work well for girls. At the same time, you can have a lot of fun with hair with the right song. Spikes, pompadours, bouffants, and funky braids might create the perfect look for a performance when you don't have the extra cash flow to create elaborate backdrops or settings.

Go All Out

Sound Vibrations, from Hart High School in Newhall, California, once created a seventeen-minute competition set based on a single theatrical concept. They were the marionettes in the "Lonely Goatherd" scene from the movie *The Sound of Music*.

The idea: they were rebelling against the puppet master who was controlling their actions. By the end of the performance, the puppets had cut their strings to set themselves free.

These performers tossed aside any self-consciousness and had fun with their makeup. To mimic the look of a puppet's mouth, they drew lines from one corner of their lips, down along their chins and up to the other corner. They painted large pink and red circles on their cheeks, darkened their brows and arched them higher up onto their foreheads. The girls and some of the boys wore long false eyelashes and drew thick bottom lashes down to nearly their cheekbones. Some made their hair into wild spikes or tangled messes, like an old doll found at the bottom of a toy box. The makeup truly made them look like a band of angry puppets.

So have fun with your makeup and your hair if it works for the performance you want to give. It's an inexpensive way to create drama and mood. Plus, it feels like Halloween every day. Who doesn't like to play dress up?

CHAPTER 3

SETS

The right sets and backdrops can create an amazing visual treat to accompany the vocal performance onstage. You don't want to crowd out or overshadow your singers with elaborate sets. The audience doesn't need to feel like it's seeing a fully staged theatrical play or Broadway musical. The focus should always be on the vocal performance. But that extra touch of a well-placed backdrop or other visual treat will create a truly enjoyable experience.

How much of these extras you include depends upon the number of glee club members onstage at any given time. For larger groups, you might need something as simple as a light show and risers to create a sense of heights and valleys for the singers to move upon. Smaller groups can have more flexibility with three-dimensional sets.

Basic Black

The black box theater grew in popularity in the 1960s. It was a minimalistic approach to art that ensured a space didn't compete with or overwhelm the performance it was supposed to house. Often, a black box theater is a large square room with black walls and ceiling and sometimes a black floor. Black box

The simplicity of a black box theater ensures all eyes focus on the performance. Its layout creates intimacy, too, pushing the audience closer to the performers. Choirs can connect more easily with the audience.

theaters offer a flexibility not found in traditional auditoriums. The neutral black doesn't clash with costumes, backdrops, and performers. Instead of auditorium seating, this style of theater usually has a flat floor that is wide open. Directors can situate the seating so that an audience gets the maximum experience from the performance. This opens up a wider variety of choreography choices.

Show choirs can have a lot of fun staging a performance for a black box theater. You can easily adapt any choreography and performance to any space. Most show choir competitions are held in traditional auditoriums, with tiered seating, curtains, and a raised stage, but show choirs often also perform in hotel ballrooms, malls, retirement communities, classrooms, and so on, especially if the group performs for outside groups to raise funds.

Creating choreography to work in a black box theater lets your group adapt to any situation, which means you can shine your brightest wherever you sing. You can also make the audience part of the set. Place the chairs in a pattern that performers can dance through. The choreography stays fluid as the audience becomes part of the show. You can even plant performers in the audience who look like they are just there for the show, until they jump up in song. It's exactly what makes a flash mob so much fun. It's the unnoticed spectator suddenly busting all the right moves with the rest of the dancers.

Low-Cost Options

Traditional large auditoriums have the advantage of larger stage space, including a backstage area to quickly move set

Eye-catching sets don't have to eat up a choir budget. Get creative by scouring your city. Theater groups regularly clean house and sell old props. Imagination and a steady hand with a glue gun can turn trash into treasure.

pieces off of and onto the stage. You still have flexibility with set design in an auditorium as well.

Your set doesn't need to be elaborate or expensive, especially if you have a tight budget or a school with limited staging accessories. String up long strips of flowing fabric behind the singers. Weight the bottom hems with wooden dowels or metal rods, or sew in small weights. Use an oscillating fan with a quiet motor set on a low speed to create subtle waves. If the song needs a heavier or more solid backdrop, you can paint inexpensive canvas panels.

LOSING IT WITH SERRANO HIGH SCHOOL, PHELAN, CALIFORNIA

Highly competitive groups put intense effort into creating nearly twenty-minute-long competition concept performances, complete with elaborate costumes, makeup, and sets as needed.

In the 2010 Show Choir Extravaganza, hosted by Los Alamitos High School's show choir, Serrano High School's Vocal Point performed a series of songs set against the backdrop of a mental hospital. The curtains rose, and the singers started to sing the first soft notes of "Mad World" by Tears for Fears. They stood on risers in front of two floating backdrops that looked like giant padded walls. The costumes were equally simple: plain black pants and white T-shirts for the boys, white tanks and sequined black knee-high skirts for the girls. It created a stark look for the stark pain in the song's lyrics and chords.

The finale found the entire choir trapped in white straight jackets, performing a choreographed spasm of arm jerks, leg kicks, and swaying torsos to the Cranberries' "Zombie." Cold bluish light seemed to glow from padded walls. The look was chilling—and the performance was dazzling enough to earn the Vocal Point singers first place in the small choir division.

Also don't forget to recycle and reuse! Scour local flea markets, Goodwill stores, even neighborhood yard sales for inexpensive pieces that suit a particular song. Benches, like risers, make flexible settings for singers.

Another inexpensive, fun set: simple large boxes painted black or whatever color complements costumes. These work especially well when incorporated with your choreography.

Paint sturdy wooden boxes black on one side, then paint a different object—for example, a body, a building, or even a car—on each of the other sides. If put on locking casters, they can roll around within choreography or be used to create height (locking casters lock when weight is put on them).

Or forgo the staging benefits of sturdy wood boxes and go with cardboard! This option can be fun as the singers lift seemingly heavy boulders, buildings, cars, whatever, over their heads—or knock them down. Just be careful not to damage the boxes, and plan to have a few multiple backups ready in case of an accident.

FAMOUS GLEEKS

What do actors Ashton Kutcher, Glenn Close, and Blake Lively have in common with singers Jason Mraz, Kimberly Wyatt, and Lance Bass? Aside from earning significantly more income than the average person, they all performed in show choir! Close was a member of the touring group Up With People, while the others performed with their high school show choirs. Lively performed in In Sync, the award-winning choir from Burbank High School in Burbank, California—not to be confused with Bass's former boy band, 'N Sync.

Traditional glee clubs can boast their own famous formers. Cole Porter wrote more than three hundred songs while singing with the Yale Glee Club. Harvard troubadours include presidents Theodore Roosevelt and Franklin D. Roosevelt and composer Leonard Bernstein. And before he became a neurosurgeon, then a CNN correspondent, Dr. Sanjay Gupta sang gleefully with the men of University of Michigan.

If your high school offers vocational technology courses, you can team up with the teachers. The vo-tech students can help build specific sets. They'll get to design and build credit, and you'll get custom-built sets. Share the cost on the materials to make it affordable for everyone.

Greece Athena High School in Rochester, New York, is a two-time National Show Choir champion. They performed the operatic "Prelude/Virtuoso" with five giant gilded rectangular frames as their set. Two of the frames were finished completely and placed on a platform with casters. These frames could be wheeled and spun, an integral part of the choreography. During certain parts of the song, one singer stood frozen in each frame.

Go High-Tech for Less

One of the easiest sets to create is also one of the most flexible and striking backdrops. In most high schools, the technology is already there. It's simply a matter of knowing how to pull it altogether and use it effectively.

VJing is a form of real-time visual art. A VJer uses multimedia to synchronize video, lights, and even a live camera to turn a simple musical performance into a higher artistic experience. Adding moving visuals into the performance creates a wholly new dramatic live concert experience.

But even a simple slide show can work, if the speed complements the pace of the songs. PowerPoint isn't just a standard software program used by teachers, principals, and guest speakers who talk to you at assemblies. A well-designed, creative PowerPoint presentation can tell a story in simple or

Most audience members have no clue about all the work done behind the scenes. This light board is an essential tool for a show choir. A savvy tech whiz with a good eye can frame a performance just by playing with the lights.

complex images. All you need is a large screen, a laptop or USB drive, a powerful monitor, and a creative content provider. PowerPoint slide shows eliminate the need to have a VJ working on site during the performance.

Tap the interests and experiences of other students to help you create amazing sets for your ideas. Start-up choirs have a unique flexibility. You don't have a preconceived idea of how your group should look or perform. You can create anything you want. If it doesn't work, no problem. Try a new idea. Then another. Then another. It's all about creating something dynamic and evolving—and having a blast while doing it.

CHAPTER 4

PROPS

Props can turn a clever performance into a stunning artistic or emotional experience—or they can backfire spectacularly into a disastrous distraction. Someone bonks another singer in the face with a prop. One trips over it while trying to glide down a riser. A handoff fails, and two singers fumble to retrieve it. Sometimes it just rolls away, lost under a riser until the last note is sung.

It's best to keep props simple and use them only when it's necessary to make a strong point. That isn't to say you can't have fun. In Newhall, California, Unleashed is the name of Hart High School's all-male show choir. They performed a brilliantly

Traditionally, glee clubs were all-male choirs. They sang short, often joyful songs — hence the name "glee." Modern choirs tend to be a mix of male and female singers, but many schools still feature all-male or all-female groups.

awkward set that started with Huey Lewis and the News' 1980s romp "Hip to Be Square." They wore white button-down shirts, heavy black-framed glasses, and a variety of children's backpacks (worn correctly, of course, with the straps securely around the shoulders). One member even sported a furry yellow Pikachu-shaped pack.

Their singing segued into rapper T-Pain's "Crazy for You/ Dance Like Me" and Cee Lo Green's remake of the Carl Douglas classic "Kung Fu Fighting," while they robot-armed their way through the choreography. The men eventually dumped their backpacks and horn-rims and stripped out of their white button-downs to reveal their black T-shirts and true ninja nature.

The songs may have been entertaining with the horn-rims and white button-downs alone, but the backpacks made the entire scene. No need for a backdrop or light show when you have twenty boys in *Star Wars* or anime backpacks clomping their way through the performance. In this case, the props made the entire show.

Low Cost, High Impact

Sometimes simple props can be effective, especially if your budget leaves little left over for elaborate costumes or cutting-edge multimedia and video displays. The best props play a crucial role in the choreography. When deciding what kinds and how many props to use, first consider why you need them. Will they create action or movement? Create a visual sense of tempo? Cause a laugh? Bring a tear?

Hand-held props must be easy to grasp, light enough to not wear out a singer after lifting and swinging arms for twenty minutes, and small enough that they won't block out a singer in the back. Larger props must also be lightweight and easily moved about. Most important, props should never take the focus away from the performer. The audience wants to see the singers' expressions and emotions pouring out of their faces.

Clothing props such as hats, canes, and capes should have a purpose beyond creating a look. Use veils, baseball caps, and other props that might cover the face sparingly and only for a specific effect.

Some simple prop ideas that work with a limited budget:

1. Attach ribbons to wooden dowels or even rulers to make inexpensive flags or streamers. The wooden handles make it easy to pass from one singer to another.

2. Paint props with glow-in-the-dark paint, then turn off the lights during a performance. You can also use glow-in-the-dark makeup, hair spray, and iron-ons. Make sure you rehearse to see how much paint you need to get the perfect effect.

3. Singers can hold the ends of long scarves to create a loop or a wave as they move through their choreography.

4. Hem and trim large pieces of cloth for multiple uses. They can act as drapes to highlight a soloist or as a privacy screen to hide or silhouette a singer. Several performers can hold one up as a sail, parachute, shelter from a storm—whatever you can picture in your imagination.

5. Foam core—that lightweight, white, cardboard-type material—is relatively inexpensive compared to buying props. If you have a steady hand or a friend with one, you can easily cut out and construct sheets of foam core into whatever you need it to be: an open umbrella, airplanes, pagodas, an elephant, a barrel of monkeys, even a robot.

6. Turn off the lights and turn on the flashlights. Tape colored gels over the lights for an even more dramatic effect.

Again, it's all about having fun. As with costumes and sets, tap the talents of other students in your school. Ask the art department to create unique props that suit your songs. Raid your closets and storage units. Approach props with a clear, open mind.

GLEE REALITY

The Fox television hit *Glee* has become so huge that it has spun off a new show. Creator and executive producer Ryan Murphy has said he wants to keep *Glee* real, which means students age in real time, graduate when they should, and leave Mr. Schuester and New Directions behind to enter into adulthood.

That mandate means Murphy must add new cast members each year and find replacements for the biggest voices who've graduated. Instead of just contacting agents, Murphy created yet another show.

Fans love the Fox television show *Glee* so much that its producers created a spin-off show. *The Glee Project* is a reality contest to choose guest cast members. Auditions for its second season started in November 2011.

The Glee Project debuted on June 12, 2011, on the cable channel Oxygen. It was a pinch of *American Idol*, a dash of *Survivor*, and nothing from *Jersey Shore*.

Tens of thousands of aspiring singers and actors flocked to its auditions with hopes of winning a seven-story arc guest spot on the show *Glee*, and possibly an invite to become a full-time cast member. After narrowing the field down to twelve finalists, the show started in earnest.

Each week the chosen few were given an assignment. The first was given by *Glee* star Darren Criss: create a character and give it a "Most Likely to" label, like you might find in a high school yearbook. The actors were to perform in that character. They filmed a group video. Producer Robert Ulrich, choreographer Zach Woodlee, and vocal coach Nikki Anders chose the bottom three performers. Those three had to re-audition for Murphy. Only two would be called back.

The formula continued thusly for the remaining hopefuls: receive an assignment based on a theme, such as individuality, theatricality, and vulnerability. Sing as a group before a guest *Glee* cast member, who then chooses a winner for a one-on-one tutoring session. Film a video in character. The bottom three must re-audition.

The show was a hit and made stars of a few fan favorites. And in the end, Murphy found there couldn't be just one. It was too hard to choose. The final four were all invited to appear on *Glee*.

Flash with Substance

Like costumes, props should enhance the unified feel of a performance. They should complete the backdrop or set and not overshadow the costumes or singers. And sometimes, the right amount of razzle-dazzle is the perfect prop, the proverbial icing on the cake.

Take the award-winning John Burroughs High School in Burbank, California. When their mixed show choir performed Katy Perry's "Firework," the choir members entered the stage amid crawling fog from a fog machine. Each student was dressed in silver. The boys wore white vests; the girls had gold floor-length trains attached to their skirts and wide sparkling gold cummerbunds.

It was a striking effect. They danced around and sang the opening lines of the song while the Death Star battle scene from *Star Wars: A New Hope* played across six column monitors in the back.

But the best part occurred halfway through the song. Both the monitors and the stage lights suddenly went black. The singers turned on their until-that-moment-unnoticed LED rings. The dancers, spread out upon the risers, used their arms to mimic an explosion of fireworks. Each time, the crowds went crazy with cheers and applause.

The effect would have been equally impressive had the singers been in jeans and hoodies in a classroom. Again, it is the unexpected prop that once you see it in action, you realize there really is no other way to properly do it. Light-emitting diode rings as fireworks. Of course!

Many show choirs channel their inner Katy Perry. It's easy to interpret her strong alto vocal range, catchy pop tunes, and dramatic flair into a choir showcase. Show choirs across the nation have sung her hit song "Firework."

Tap into your creativity. Look at what other show choirs have done with relatively inexpensive choices. What can you do? Silly backpacks. Children-sized umbrellas. Hard hats and canes. Ribbons and dowels.

What is easy to hold, easy to pass, and lightweight enough to carry and swing for up to twenty minutes? What does the song need, if anything? Will it cause the reaction you want from your audience? Will they gasp with delight, laugh out loud at your clever humor, feel that pang of angst or melancholy? If it doesn't complete the performance, consider dropping the prop.

CHAPTER 5

THE PERFORMANCE

The sets are built. The props are in place. The costumes and makeup are perfect. You walk through a darkened backstage, past dressing rooms, over ropes, and under rigging. You reach the stage, find your place on the riser, and strike your pose. You steady your breath, swallow one last time, hope your top lip doesn't stick to your front teeth. You've agonized over complex dance steps and memorized the notes and words for your part. It's come to one moment, this moment, and it can't come fast enough.

The lights suddenly flash on like a silent explosion in your face. The director's arm rises. A deep breath and…

Show choirs put hours into rehearsals. Weeks of clumsy dance steps, aching muscles, and vocal exercises meld into the final moment: the performance. Being onstage feels like nothing else in the world. Thrilling. Terrifying. Energizing.

It's showtime!

This is the moment you've prepared for. And the first time is never what you expect it to be.

People might want to join a vocal group or glee club thinking it will be like the television program. But television doesn't always reflect reality. Singers don't just break out into perfect pitch song and dance at rehearsal, with a ready-made band popping into place as if the Keebler elf zapped them there.

It takes hours of practice. Each day. For weeks. And months. The award-winning Arcadia High School from

Arcadia, California, practices eighteen hours a week. In some of the more competitive, illustrious choirs, you have to audition—and not everyone makes it. Dozens of Greece Athena High School show choir alumni have gone on to perform on Broadway. Each year, hundreds audition for a coveted spot in that school's show choir. Only one in ten makes it.

Once they're in, show choir members can't coast. Most high schools enforce academic requirements. In other words, you have to perform academically or else you can't perform vocally.

Cutthroat Competition

If you watch television programs about show choir competitions, you might come away with the impression that it is brutal, ugly, and devious.

Sure, it can be that way. But for most choirs, it truly is a once-in-a-lifetime experience and loads of fun. There are several regional competitions and a few national biggies, such as FAME Show Choir Championships, Finale National Show Choir Championships, and Show Choir Nationals. These competitions draw hundreds of hopefuls eager to earn the right to call themselves national champions. But unlike the Super Bowl, the World Series, or the World Cup, there isn't a governing body established to officially name a singular champ.

Still, competitions give you the chance to perform against other schools, to see what they do well and discover what might not work so well in your group. Regardless of how you place, you will learn so much from the experience.

CASH FLOW

School arts budgets face brutal cuts each year. Strapped parents find less in their pockets to dole out for extracurricular activities. You need some creative fund-raising ideas. Jump-start your brainstorming with the following ideas:

1. Singing telegrams: Get permission from your school principal first, and set up an action plan: will you deliver telegrams at the start of class or in the hallway at the end of class? Will they be delivered during lunch? Smaller schools might be able to pull them off at the beginning of the day while students are streaming in to the common areas. Valentine's Day alone can bring in some serious dough.

2. Serenading car washes: Sing while you soap! You can even choreograph moves during the wash/rinse/dry cycle.

3. Digital downloads: Create a video and post it to your Web site and social media pages. Add a link where folks can get digital downloads for a small donation. Ninety-nine cents might not sound like it's worth the time and effort to set up this plan, but you'll be surprised at how many video hits you get—and how many opt for the download.

4. Burn a CD or DVD: Once you get enough performances down tight, burn a CD or DVD and sell it wherever you go. Your aunties and uncles want to support you, so hit them up!

5. Personalized ringtones: Really, do we need to say anything here? Teens love changing it up, and a fresh ringtone each week is exactly what they want, especially when their talented friends are doing the crooning.

6. Team up: Join forces with the band, dance squad, or any other group that needs funds. Often, fund-raising companies offer profit percentages based on volume sold. The more cookie dough you move, the more money per order you earn.

7. Make concessions: People scoff at stores that charge high rates for drinks and snacks. But for some reason, once they're at a sporting event, they pay twice and three times as much for water, candy, pizza, and pretzels without flinching. Most high schools have some kind of fund-raising arrangement in place with student groups and parent boosters clubs. Tap into it.

Offstage Glee

Modern technology means glee clubs and show choirs aren't restricted to theaters and auditoriums, or even shopping malls. Want to get your performance before the masses? Do what Johns Creek High School in Johns Creek, Georgia, did to promote their group, newly formed for the 2010–2011 school year.

They staged a video shoot in a classroom, featuring singers performing a mashup of Sean Kingston's "Beautiful Girls" with Ben E. King's R&B classic "Stand by Me." Then they posted it on YouTube.

You have multiple creative routes to travel if you want to try filming mini movies out of your performances. You can change locations, change out singers, dance in any space, add special

Show choirs tap all sources to create musical mashups. The students at Johns Creek High School in Johns Creek, Georgia, mashed hits by rhythm and blues legend Ben E. King with the young Jamaican American singer Sean Kingston.

effects, and maintain the continuity. You can showcase fancy footwork, strong soloists, and every member's personality with close-ups—one thing that is impossible to achieve onstage in a large group.

Videos are great promotional pieces for competition, fund-raising, and just getting people excited about an upcoming show. Your high school likely has a television course. Hook up with the teacher and students to create your video. Who knows? It could go viral.

Curtain Calls

Yes, show choir takes intense drive, a huge time commitment, lots of sweat, lots of tears, and sometimes a little bit of blood.

But it's so, so worth it.

Broadway star Donna Lynne Champlin, an alumna of Athena High Show, described it like this in the documentary *Gleeful: The Real Show Choirs of America*:

"Show choir for me was not only learning how to perform with other people and solos and a cappella singing. It was a grab bag of performing experience. I knew how to audition for things because I had to audition. I audition every day. There's nothing about show choir that has not helped me in what I do now."

So go make your dreams come true, and shine on!

GLOSSARY

a cappella One or more vocalists performing without an instrumental accompaniment.

choreography Coordinated dance moves that tell a story.

chorus A group singing in unison.

flash mob A group of people, usually dozens or more, who break out into a musical or dramatic performance in the middle of a public place.

glee Historically, a short song sung by a trio or quartet of men and occasionally mixed groups of men and women.

juxtaposition The act of putting two or more things together. The term is used often when the elements contrast.

mashup A musical performance that combines two seemingly disparate pieces of music into one smooth, cohesive song.

pompadour A hairstyle where the front of the hair is styled into a high mound.

riser A platform, usually with multiple elevations, used by choruses onstage to ensure the audience sees each singer.

show choir A vocal group that performs modern pop songs and incorporates dance moves.

spats A men's shoe style whereby a piece of cloth covers the top part of the foot, the instep, and the ankle.

unison Two or more singers performing the same notes and melody at the same pitch or in different octaves.

FOR MORE INFORMATION

American Choral Directors Association
545 Couch Drive
Oklahoma City, OK 73102-2207
(405) 232-8161
Web site: http://acda.org
Founded in 1959, the American Choral Directors Association
(ACDA) is a nonprofit music-education organization whose
central purpose is to promote excellence in choral music
through performance, composition, publication, research,
and teaching. In addition, the ACDA strives through arts
advocacy to elevate choral music's position in society.

Princeton University Glee Club
Department of Music
Woolworth Music Center
Princeton University
Princeton, NJ 08544
Web site http://webscript.princeton.edu/~gleeclub/index.php
Princeton's oldest choir, the Glee Club, is composed of about sixty-
five mixed voices and gives multiple performances throughout
the year, featuring music from the Renaissance to the present
day. The Glee Club tours internationally every two years.
International tours have included locations as diverse as Italy,
Hong Kong, and Buenos Aires.

Showchoir Camps of America
P.O. Box 583
Naperville, IL 60566
(630) 663-4500
Web site: http://www.showchoircamps.com
The group offers camps for junior high and high school students,
as well as music teachers and choral directors at Millikin

University in Decatur, Illinois, and Heidelberg University in Tiffin, Ohio. Showchoir Camps of America encourage high standards of excellence while having lots of fun with people from around the world.

Show Choir Canada
736 Bathurst Street
Toronto, ON M5S 2R4
Canada
(877) 90GLEEK (904-5335), ext. 227
Web site: http://www.showchoircanada.com
Show Choir Canada aims to play a vital role in the development and support of show choirs by creating opportunities that inspire youth participants to work together through song and dance. It strives to help youth achieve excellence as a group and as individuals while sharing in the creative process.

Show Choir Nationals
3317 Winchester Road
Birmingham, AL 35226
(205) 305-8543
Web site: http://www.showchoirnationals.com
Show Choir Nationals aims to gather elite, competitive groups from across the country so that every participant learns from performing and watching other excellent performers. Judges are current educators who have worked with show choirs themselves or have remained active in judging.

The Singing Hoosiers
Indiana University Jacobs School of Music
Office of Musical Attractions

1201 E. Third Street
Bloomington, IN 47405-7006
(812) 855-7047
Founded in 1950, the Singing Hoosiers feature about 115 col-
legiate performers from the world-renown Indiana University
Jacobs School of Music, as well as students with a variety of
other majors. They perform American popular music, jazz,
and Broadway favorites with dazzling choreography, energy,
and style.

University of Notre Dame Glee Club
Crowley Hall of Music
University of Notre Dame
Notre Dame, IN 46556
(574) 631-6352
Web site: http://gleeclub.nd.edu
The Notre Dame Glee Club continues the musical tradition that
began in 1915. Drawing on a wide repertoire of music from
ancient polyphony to modern pieces, the all-male Glee Club
entertains thousands of fans around the country and the world
every year.

Utah Glee Club
(801) 369-5680
Web site: http://utahgleeclub.com
The group is comprised of twelve- to eighteen-year-old singers who
perform benefit concerts for local arts programs. The Utah
Glee Club aims to generate fund-raising and enhance com-
munication among arts groups and the general public by
performing regular concerts and sponsored events.

Yale Glee Club
201 Hendrie Hall
165 Elm Street
New Haven, CT 06520
(203) 432-4136
Web site: http://www.yalegleeclub.org
This eighty-voice chorus of women and men perform a repertoire
    that embraces a broad spectrum of choral music from the
    sixteenth century to the present, including Renaissance motets,
    contemporary choral works, folk music, spirituals, and tradi-
    tional Yale songs.

Web Sites

Due to the changing nature of Internet links, Rosen Publishing
has developed an online list of Web sites related to the subject
of this book. This site is updated regularly. Please use this link
to access the list:

http://www.rosenlinks.com/glee/style

FOR FURTHER READING

Anders, Susan. *Singing Live: The Performing Skills Guidebook for Contemporary Singers*. Kindle version. Zanna Discs, 2958-6 edition, 2008.

Bailey, Diane. *Scenery and Set Designs* (High School Musicals). New York, NY: Rosen Central, 2009.

Brunetti, David. *Acting Songs*. Charleston, SC: Book Surge Publishing, 2006.

Carver, Rita Kogler. *Stagecraft Fundamentals: A Guide and Reference for Theatrical Production*. Waltham, MA: Focal Press, 2008.

Gillette, J. Michael. *Theatrical Design and Production: An Introduction to Scenic Design and Construction, Lighting, Sound, Costume, and Makeup*. New York, NY: McGraw-Hill Humanities/Social Sciences/Languages, 2007.

Jameson, Gladys. *The School Glee Club: Standard Classics and Folk Music in Easy Arrangements for Male Voices*. Rockville, MD: Wildside Press, 2008.

LaBouff, Kathryn. *Singing and Communicating in English: A Singer's Guide to English Diction*. New York, NY: Oxford University Press, 2007.

Mack, Valerie Lippoldt. *Putting the SHOW in CHOIR: The Ultimate Handbook for Your Rehearsal and Performance*. New York, NY: Shawnee Press, 2011.

Ostwald, David. *Acting for Singers: Creating Believable Singing Characters*. New York, NY: Oxford University Press, 2005.

Parker, W. Oren, R. Craig Wolf, and Dick Block. *Scene Design and Stage Lighting*. Florence, KY: Wadsworth Publishing, 2008.

Seelig, Timothy. *The Perfect Blend: Seriously Fun Vocal Warm Ups*. New York, NY: Shawnee Press, 2005.

Shelley, Steven Louis. *A Practical Guide to Stage Lighting*. Waltham, MA: Focal Press, 2009.

Svitil, Torene. *So You Want to Work in Set Design, Costuming, or Make-up?* Berkeley Heights, NJ: Enslow Publishers, 2008.

Ward, Charlotte. *The Official Glee Annual 2011.* London, England: Headline Publishing Group, 2010.

Weaver, Mike. *Sweat, Tears, and Jazz Hands: The Official History of Show Choir from Vaudeville to Glee.* Milwaukee, WI: Hal Leonard, 2011.

BIBLIOGRAPHY

Campbell, Drew. *Technical Theater for Nontechnical People*. New York, NY: Allworth Press, 2004.

Dion, Christine. *High Performance Beauty: Makeup & Skin Care for Dance, Cheer, Show Choir, Pageants & Ice Skating*. Hightstown, NJ: Princeton Book Company, 2007.

Donathan, David. *How Does Your Choir Grow?* Nashville, TN: Abingdon Press, 1995.

GleeClubUK.com. "What Is a Glee Club?" Retrieved October 11, 2011 (http://www.gleeclubuk.com/home/what_is_a _glee_club.aspx).

Gleeful: The Real American Glee Club. Channel 4 documentary. Retrieved October 9, 2011 (http://www.channel4.com/ programmes/gleeful-the-real-show-choirs-of-america)

Häakon. "New Book Chronicles the History of Show Choir in Extraordinary Detail." ShowChoir.com, August 2, 2011. Retrieved October 9, 2011 (http://www.showchoir.com/ index.php?ar=11).

HarvardGleeClub.com "History of Harvard Glee Club." Retrieved October 7, 2011 (http://www.harvardgleeclub.org/info/ history).

Johnson, Neil. "Popularity of Show Choirs Is Growing in Local High Schools." GazetteXtra.com, January 31, 2011. Retrieved October 9, 2011 (http:// gazettextra.com/news/2011/jan/31/ popularity-show-choirs-growing-local-high-schools).

Kaluta, John. *The Perfect Stage Crew: The Compleat Technical Guide for High School, College and Community Theater*. New York, NY: Allworth Press, 2003.

Litherland, Janet, Sue McAnally, and Michelle Gallardo. *Broadway Costumes on a Budget*. Colorado Springs, CO: Meriwether Publishing, Ltd., 1996.

Loomis, George Brace. *The Progressive Glee and Chorus Book*.

Charleston, SC: BiblioBazaar, 2009.

Lynch, Tom. "Preview: The Blue Ribbon Glee Club/Empty Bottle." NewCityMusic.com, January 5, 2009. Retrieved October 11, 2011 (http://music.newcity.com/2009/01/05/preview-the-blue-ribbon-glee-clubempty-bottle).

Mack, Valerie Lippoldt. *Putting the SHOW in CHOIR: The Ultimate Handbook for Your Rehearsal and Performance*. New York, NY: Shawnee Press, 2011.

Montgomery, Bruce. *Brothers, Sing On!: My Half-Century Around the World with the Penn Glee Club*. Philadelphia, PA: University of Pennsylvania Press, 2005.

Peel, Sarah. "The Glee Project Gets Green Light for Second Season." BSCKids.com, September 29, 2011. Retrieved October 9, 2011 (http://www.bsckids.com/2011/09/the-glee-project-gets-green-light-for-second-season).

Prevost, Michel. "Hitting All the Right Notes." *The Tabaret: The Magazine of the University of Ottawa*. Retrieved October 9, 2011 (http://www.tabaret.uottawa.ca/article_e_395.html).

Princ, Lisa. "The Glee Project Casting for the Next Season." RealityTVmagazine.com, September 27, 2011. Retrieved October 8, 2011 (http://realitytvmagazine.sheknows.com/2011/09/27/the-glee-project-casting-for-the-next-season).

Raoul, Bill. *Stock Scenery Construction: A Handbook*. Louisville, KY: Broadway Press, 1998.

Rocca, Mo. "Real Life Glee." *CBS Sunday Morning*, January 8, 2009. Retrieved October 11, 2011 (http://www.youtube.com/watch?v=pKlfKl8QU4k&feature=related).

Rogers, Barb. *Costuming Made Easy: How to Make Theatrical Costumes from Cast-off Clothing*. Colorado Springs, CO: Meriwether Publishing, 1999.

Sobel, Liza. "Glee Club Triumphs." *Cornell Daily Sun*, September

20, 2011. Retrieved October 8, 2011 (http://www
.cornellsun.com/section/arts/content/2011/09/20/
glee-club-triumphs).

Swinfield, Rosemarie. *Stage Makeup Step-by-Step*. Cincinnati,
OH: Betterway Books, 1995.

Thudium, Laura. *Stage Makeup: The Actor's Complete Guide to
Today's Techniques and Materials*. New York, NY: Back
Stage Books, 1999.

Weaver, Mike. *Sweat, Tears, and Jazz Hands: The Official History
of Show Choir from Vaudeville to Glee*. Milwaukee, WI: Hal
Leonard, 2011.

Winterman, Denise. "For the Love of Glee." *BBC News
Magazine*, January 22, 2010. Retrieved October 9, 2011
(http://news.bbc.co.uk/2/hi/uk_news/
magazine/8469886.stm).

INDEX

A

Arcadia High School show choir, 46–47

B

black box theaters, 28–29
Blue Ribbon Glee Club, 21

C

competitions, 47
costumes, 7–16
  basic uniform, 8–11
  creating/embellishing, 16
  and ease of movement, 7–8
  and expenses, 6, 16
  and flattering all body types, 8, 9, 10
  importance of, 7
  and simple, unified look, 11, 13–14
  and theme, 11–13
  and the unexpected, 15–16

F

fund-raising, 48–49, 51

G

Glee (TV show), 4, 11, 14–15, 40–41
glee clubs/show choirs
  about modern, 4–6
  and competitions, 47
  and costumes, 7–16
  and expenses, 6, 16
  famous members of, 32
  fund-raising for, 48–49, 51
  history of, 4, 10, 14, 19

and makeup, 17–26
and the performance, 45–51
and props, 36–44
and sets, 27–35
and travel, 6
Glee Project, The (TV show), 40–41
Greece Athena High School show choir, 15–16, 33, 47

H

hairstyles, 25
Harrow School, 14
Hart High School show choir, 25–26, 36–38
Harvard Glee Club, 10, 19

I

Immaculate Conception Academy show choir, 11–13

J

John Burroughs High School show choir, 20, 42
Johns Creek High School glee club, 6, 49

M

makeup, 17–26
  dramatic, 20
  for the eyes, 22–23
  importance of, 17–20, 26
  for the lips, 23–25
  natural look, 20–21
Murphy, Ryan, 40–41

O

Olentangy High School show choir, 11

P

props, 36–44
  low-cost, 38–39

S

Serrano High School show choir, 31
sets, 27–35
  black box theaters, 28–29
  importance of, 27–28
  low-cost options, 29–33

using technology for, 33–35
show choir, about modern, 4–6

V

videos, filming, 49–51
VJing, 33

W

Wheaton Warrenville High School show
  choir, 13

Y

YouTube, posting videos to, 6, 49

About the Author

Colleen Ryckert Cook writes nonfiction for children, teens, and adults. She lives in Kansas.

Photo Credits

Cover (teenage girls) Jupiterimages/Brand X Pictures/Thinkstock, (spotlight) © istockphoto.com/evirgen, (make-up kit) © www.istockphoto.com/Kae Horng Mau; cover, back cover, interior graphics (stars, lit frame) © www.istockphoto.com/Yap Siew Hoong; back cover, interior graphics (stage lights silhouette) Collina/Shutterstock.com; p. 5 muzsy/Shutterstock.com; pp. 9, 37 Photo Researchers/Getty Images; p. 12 © Bob Daemmrich/PhotoEdit; p. 15 Hill Street Studios/Blend Images/Getty Images; p. 18 © www.istockphoto.com/Igor Demchenkov; p. 22 tan4ikk/Shutterstock.com; p. 24 Olinchuk/Shutterstock.com; p. 28 © Mark Rightmire/The Orange County Register/ZUMApress.com; p. 30 godrick/Shutterstock.com; p. 34 iStockphoto/Thinkstock; p. 40 © Nancy Kaszerman/ZUMApress.com; p. 43 George Napolitano/FilmMagic/Getty Images; p. 46 © St. Petersburg Times/ZUMApress.com; p. 50 Michael Ochs Archives/Getty Images.

Designer: Nicole Russo; Editor: Bethany Bryan;
Photo Researcher: Karen Huang

64